Tin and the Bolivian Economy

DAVID J. FOX, B.Sc., M.A.

Lecturer in Geography at the University of Manchester

LATIN AMERICAN PUBLICATIONS FUND
31 TAVISTOCK SQUARE
LONDON W.C.1.

1970

Published by Latin American Publications Fund, Copyright 1970.
Printed by The Hove Printing Company, Hove, Sussex, England.

Standard Book Number 9500787 1 9

Contents

Centre Pages

DAVID J. FOX

David Fox, B.Sc., M.A., is a lecturer in Geography at the University of Manchester. He shares an interest in tin with his father, who is Secretary of the International Tin Council. He first became concerned with mining problems while attached to McGill University's Sub-Arctic Research Laboratory in the iron-mining area of Labrador. His work has subsequently taken him to Latin America. At the first Technological Conference on Tin held in London in 1967, he spoke on the problems of the Bolivian tin mining industry; at the second conference in Bangkok in 1969 he presented another paper on the tin mining industry of Spain and Portugal. He has published about twenty papers in British, American and Latin American journals. The Royal Society and the Social Science Research Council are supporting further work by him on the Bolivian mining industry.

David Fox delivered a paper on Tin and the Bolivian Economy at a seminar held at the Institute of Latin American Studies, University of London, in April 1969.

Tin and the Bolivian Economy

TIN IS THE CORNERSTONE of the Bolivian economy, and practically the only thing that gives Bolivia a claim to world attention. The country accounts for about one-sixth of the total amount of tin produced in the world, being second in importance to Malaysia on this score, and is, moreover, the only major producer of tin in the hemisphere that contains the world's largest consumer. No other country is so dependent on tin: during the twentieth century about two-thirds of Bolivia's income from exports has come from this commodity.

Within Bolivia tin mining today accounts for probably about 7 per cent of the gross domestic product. This compares with 10 per cent for mining in general, 15 per cent for manufacturing and 20 per cent for agriculture. There are only about 50,000 miners in the country, however, or 3 per cent of the total work force. This number belies their significance. For example, in 1968 the average miner contributed ten times as much to the domestic economy as did the average farmer. On the political front, the tin miners are the largest body of organized labour in the country, apart from the Army, and have proved many times over the last quarter-century that they are a militant body to be reckoned with. Their support of the Movimiento Nacionalista Revolucionario (M.N.R.) in 1952 was of critical importance, and nationalization of the large mines was their reward.

Heavy reliance upon tin places Bolivia in an exposed position, made all the more vulnerable by high production costs. She is pursuing a number of policies to mitigate the adverse effects of this over-concentration. In the short run, the aim is to improve the efficiency of the industry and to encourage the exploitation of other minerals; in the long run, the aim is to diversify output and to bring a larger proportion of the country and people into the national economy. Success in meeting both these objectives will rely heavily upon income from the sale of tin: a low tin price over the next few years could be disastrous. But Bolivia has neither the technical ability nor the domestic capital to achieve her aims unassisted. Fortunately, a heightened awareness of the possible political repercussions of a destitute Bolivia and a genuine concern for the welfare of Bolivians have won Bolivia large sums of international aid during the last decade, including some on a limited scale from the United Kingdom. The hope is that this will continue into the future.

Geographical Pattern of Tin Mining

The position of the tin zone of Bolivia and the distribution of all the mines of any consequence are shown in FIGURE 2. The tin zone lies in the high Eastern Andes and extends for 800 km in a great arc southwards from Lake Titicaca; it peters out after it has crossed over the Argentine border. Tin-rich rocks form under very restricted geological circumstances and the coincidence of the tin zone, the only important accumulation of tin in South America, with the great flexure of the Andes may not be fortuitous. It is argued that dispersed tin accumulated in the deepest part of the Andean geosyncline in Palaeozoic times and that westward movement of the Brazilian Shield in Triassic times both created the flexure and concentrated the tin into mineral-rich magmas. These were subsequently injected as veins into the upper levels, producing a series of mineral-fringed granitic masses or batholiths. Later, faulting and folding was followed by a period of relaxed pressure and some of the tin was redistributed in a secondary phase of mineralization; this affected only the southern part of the zone. Uplift and broad warping in relatively recent times has exposed, in particular, the northern part of the tin zone to erosion, and the batholiths appear at the surface in the Cordillera Real; further south, less tilting occurred, the Andes remain wider and the batholiths are hidden. Recent volcanic outpourings blanket parts of the tin zone.

Tin is not the only economic mineral of the country and it is frequently found associated with, and sometimes mined in, other areas. Geologists recognize a coarse pattern in which the degree of tin-bismuth-silver mineralization declines away from the centre of the country as tungsten and antimony become more important. The detailed geology of individual regions often reveals complex sequences of mineralization with tin, sometimes with bismuth and silver, separating out after antimony and tungsten and long after gold. One of the important consequences of this association of minerals is that, despite the remarkable change in Bolivia's rôle from being one of the richest sources of silver in colonial days to its modern rôle as a world supplier of tin, the economic centre of gravity of the country has remained the same. The La Paz-Potosí axis, pivoted on Oruro, remains firmly established as the heart of the country. One-half of the tin produced in Bolivia has come from the area within 100 km of Oruro; towns like Potosí, the old silver capital, have found new life as tin mining centres.

The tin mines

Tin is mined in several ways in Bolivia. Some tin is still won from the surface, but most of it comes from underground mines unlike the situation in many tinfields. The tin zone is criss-crossed by trenches and diggings marking the outcrops of veins from which Indians may scratch a living. A little tin is mined from morainic and alluvial accumulations, although conditions are much more difficult than in the great alluvial tin fields of South-east Asia. Finally, dumps of discarded tailings from the concentrating mills provide pickings for both large-scale and individual producers. No matter which method of mining is used, the ore is low-grade, a 1 per cent tin content being quite normal, and improvement into a concentrate better able to bear shipping costs is normally done as close as possible to the source of tin. The bigger mines support their own concentrating mills; smaller producers use a variety of hand-sorting, puddling and washing methods to raise the quality of their ore.

Over 90 per cent of Bolivia's tin comes from the underground mines as in Cornwall. These vary in size. The largest (Llallagua) is producing about 2 million tons of ore a year, yielding up to 5,000 tons of tin, and five others have averaged over 1,000 tons of tin in recent years; another twenty are producing annually between 100 and 1,000 tons of tin. At the other end of the scale, there are perhaps 1,000 small producers each with an annual production of under 5 tons of tin. In 1967 the six largest mines accounted for half of the tin mined in Bolivia; these are, in order of importance, Llallagua, Potosí, Colquiri, Huanuni, Chorolque and San José de Oruro (Photographs 1a, 2a).

The Llallagua mine is the outstanding mine in Bolivia. It is, in fact, the most productive tin mine in the world. Since mining began in 1903 it has produced about 30 per cent of all Bolivia's tin, or 6 per cent of the world's tin, a total in excess of one-half million tons of tin, worth about £800 million at early-1970 prices. The mine is in difficult country, 4,400 m high near the continental divide in the high Andes. The mineralized area, as at other mines, is very small (1.0×1.4 km at the surface) and is associated with, although not exactly coterminous with, a degraded volcanic vent. The vent apparently tapers with depth and at 650 m below ground is only half its surface size. As a result of two periods of local fracturing and regional faulting, the stock and the immediate country rock are threaded by a lattice-work of tin-bearing veins. These dip steeply, become fewer with depth and are rarely longer than 700 m.; their average width lies between 30 and 80 cms. In some places, especially in the middle levels between —250 m and —450 m, 'ore shoots' consisting of hundreds of veinlets from 1 to 5 cm thick, impregnating a zone up to 5 m thick and 100-200 m long, form a sheet structure of ore grade. The nature of the ore varies with depth: essentially, it seems to be a case of high-grade cassiterite or tin oxide in the middle levels, sandwiched above and below by pyrites and marcasite. Most veins are impoverished below —650 m, although the San José vein remains mineralized to depths of —770 m.

Two methods are used to mine the ore, both very different from the vast open-cast operations in the Chilean copper mines. The traditional method (piercing the ore zone with nearly horizontal galleries accessible from shafts or adits and mining by cut-and-fill) still accounts for a substantial proportion of the ore mined. The vent rises above the local terrain and this has eased ore extraction. For example, the principal level, the Siglo XX at —650 m below the summit, is reached from an adit whose exit is 1.7 km north-east of the edge of the ore body; the higher Cancaniri (—411 m) and Patiño (—383 m) levels are reached from adits closer to the foot of the vent. In total there are about 700 km of galleries in Llallagua mine extending over a height range of 800 m in a series of levels approximately 35 m apart, but with

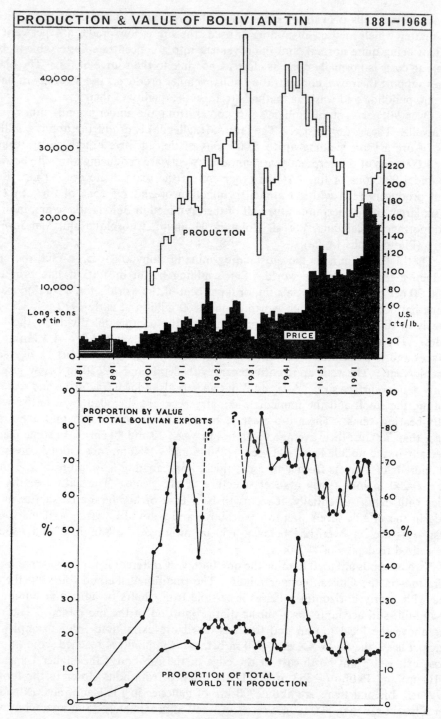

PRODUCTION & VALUE OF BOLIVIAN TIN   1881—1968

PRODUCTION

PRICE

Long tons of tin

U.S. cts/lb.

PROPORTION BY VALUE OF TOTAL BOLIVIAN EXPORTS

PROPORTION OF TOTAL WORLD TIN PRODUCTION

FIGURE 1

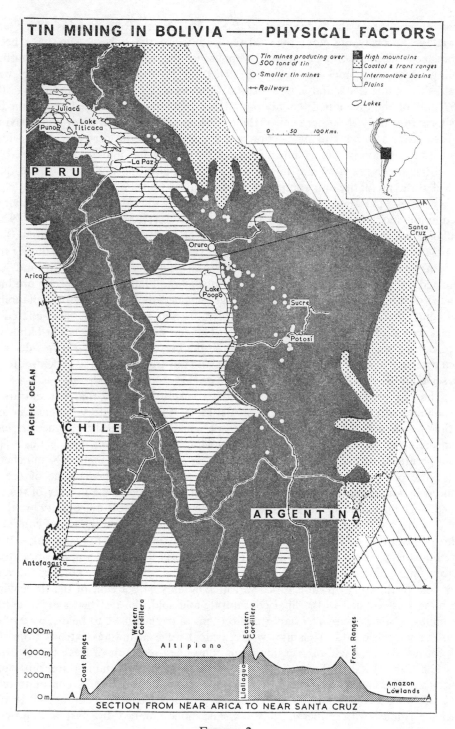

TIN MINING IN BOLIVIA —— PHYSICAL FACTORS

Tin mines producing over 500 tons of tin
Smaller tin mines
Railways

High mountains
Coastal & front ranges
Intermontane basins
Plains

Lakes

0   50   100 Kms.

PERU

Juliacá
Lake Titicaca
Puno
La Paz

Santa Cruz

Arica

Oruro

Lake Poopó

Sucre

Potosí

PACIFIC OCEAN

CHILE

ARGENTINA

Antofagasta

SECTION FROM NEAR ARICA TO NEAR SANTA CRUZ

6000m
4000m
2000m
0m

A

Coast Ranges

Western Cordillera

Altiplano

Eastern Cordillera

Llallagua

Front Ranges

Amazon Lowlands

A

FIGURE 2

5

many exceptions in the older part of the mine. Work follows veins which are nowadays normally no more than 20 cm wide since the richest veins have been exhausted. The declining quality of the ore has led the management to adopt another mining technique, block-caving. The structural feasibility of block-caving was established in the 1940s and is now the most important extractive method used. By 1957 half of the ore mined, containing 40 per cent of the tin mined, was won by block-caving; in 1962 60 per cent of the ore being processed was from block-caving and it is expected that this proportion will shortly become 80 per cent. The wide-spread substitution of bulk mining for selective mining has allowed, and caused, a reduction in the grade of ore mined and, by devaluing the definition of ore, has extended the useful life and volume of reserves of the mine.

In spite of the new lease of life given to the mine by the adoption of block-caving, production has fallen substantially over the years. At its peak in the late 1920s Llallagua was producing over 29,000 tons of tin or 45 per cent of Bolivia's total, but by 1938 production was down to 7,890 tons of tin (31 per cent). In 1951, during the Korean war, it reached 10,720 tons (30 per cent) but has since fallen off and has averaged only 4,000 tons (20 per cent) a year during the 1960s. Although tin production has declined, the amount of ore mined has remained about constant for, unhappily, Llallagua, in common with almost all other tin mines in Bolivia, has suffered a remarkable decline in the quality of ore. Gangue material used as cut-filling or discarded as spoil in one decade has become the ore of the next. Figures derived from a variety of more-or-less reliable sources and illustrated in FIGURE 3 demonstrate the scale and regularity of this decline in ore grade.

The low grade material will carry little transport costs so that concentration at the mine into higher grade material is desirable, if not mandatory. Beneficiation of the ores takes place in several stages, all designed to separate the gangue (or *cola*) from the enriched *concentrado* and each involving a degree of wastage of tin. The first operation, that of pre-concentration, is performed at the Siglo XX minehead where the ore passes through a sink-and-float plant. Here the volume of ore is reduced by about one-half but only at the cost of losing about one-quarter of the tin mined. The pre-concentrate and old tailings now of acceptable ore quality are then sent 5 km to one of two mills in Catavi, where further milling and the use of consider-able quantities of water and electricity produce a concentrate for shipping. It is here that the great change in bulk occurs; the Victoria mill, for example, works to a concentration ratio of about 50:1. Perhaps the salient feature to be noted is the very large loss in the concentration processes: in 1964 only 44 per cent of the tin leaving the mine was retained in the final concentrate and sold, the rest being discarded in the tailings. Every year over half a million tons of gangue have to be disposed of at both the minehead and at Catavi, where a great ridge of tailings extends from the mill for a full mile, itself an occasional but convenient reservoir of fresh tin reserves.

The Cerro Rico de Potosí is probably the most famous mining area in South America. The conical hill which lies south of the town (in itself a charming relic of the colonial period), and rises 700 m above it, is cored by the conduit of an old volcano, riddled with mineralized veins, and honeycombed by past and present adits and galleys.   In the sixteenth century it was the richest silver mine in the world; even with its present importance for tin the town has only one-third (50,000) of its population of three centuries ago.   The summit of the hill is at 4,790 m; most of the silver came from the upper 400 m; below this level tin became more important and mining continues to depths of 990 m below the summit.   At this depth, mining conditions became intolerably hot and exhausting.   Like other mines, however, Potosí has had to rely more and more heavily on deeper ores.   This is unfortunate not only because of the unpleasant working conditions but also because of added haulage costs and the greater complexity of the ores, notably a higher sulphide content.   Potosí suffers, more than most mines in Bolivia, from the dangers of working in an area where many of the old workings are uncharted.   It is, in fact, only since 1930 that there has been any attempt at a unified control of mining, and outmoded privileges and traditions have taken a long time to kill.   Even today some 30 per cent of the tin produced in the area comes from the 'small miners', a higher proportion than elsewhere.

Colquiri lies in open, undulating country, 4,200 m above sea level and close to the main divide.   It also began life as a silver mine and became an important tin producer only in 1938 with the completion of a road link to the railway.   Since then, 80,000 tons of tin have been shipped to Oruro and the world market.   Half the tin that is mined nowadays remains in the tailings of the concentrating mill for, as elsewhere, the grade of ore mined has declined with the years.   Huanuni has produced over 100,000 tons of tin since first worked by an English company in 1880, and it is only in the last five years that it has dropped from second place behind Llallagua. It has been a highly productive mine partly because much of the ore is in the more easily reduced oxide form and partly because much of it could be won by using adits driven into the hillside.   But the ore apparently gives out with depth and none is mined from below the 480 m level although there have been hopes of tin at greater depths.   Zinc, lead and silver have been useful impurities in the past.   San José, not far away, produces silver, lead and antimony as well as tin, and some of the workings date back to the sixteenth century.   It is one of the few mines in Bolivia to be below the 4,000 m contour line and will benefit from being close to Oruro, chosen to be the smelting centre for the country.   Chorolque is the largest tin mine in the south of the country, one of the oldest and certainly one placed in the most spectacular setting.   It takes its name from the matterhorn which rises 1,500 m above the bunch-grass ranges of the southern cordillera.   The snowy peak (5,600m) has been mined since 1870 and tin is recovered from adits down to the 4,800 m level.   Silver, wolfram and bismuth have been mined at lower levels.   Tasna, a large mine nearby and in a similar situation, held for the first thirty years of this century a virtual world monopoly of bismuth production.   Mining in the north, at Viloco and Caracoles and behind La Paz, for example, is carried out sometimes against a brilliant backcloth of alpine peaks and eternal snows at heights frequently over 5,000 m and in conditions as bleak as can be found anywhere in the world.   Such conditions not only make mining difficult: they also make road building and main-tenance expensive and travel dangerous.

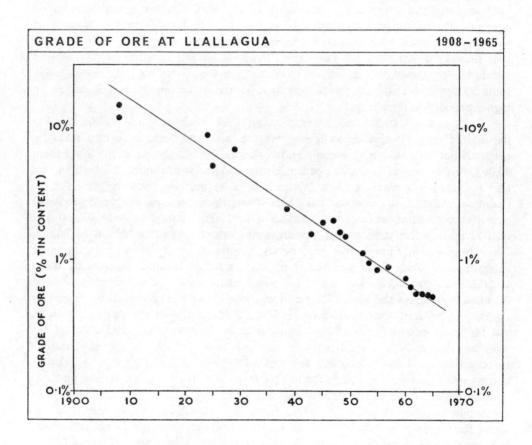

GRADE OF ORE AT LLALLAGUA   1908–1965

FIGURE 3

8

Alluvial tin mining is little practised in Bolivia. There has been some natural accumulation of tin-bearing rocks in the moraines and in the coarse alluvium brought down by the torrents that flush the tin zone. But the material is ill-sorted and quite unlike the extensive, fine-grained, easily dredged residue from tropical weathering that form the alluvial ores of Malaysia and Indonesia. In Bolivia, the debris is scattered and ranges from angular boulders weighing several tons to cassiterite dust. Many deposits are worked by individuals, a few have attracted commercial attention. Washings downstream from Potosí, at the foot of the Cordillera Quimsa Cruz (El Rodeo), behind Huanuni, and moraines near Chorolque have all been mined. The only tin dredges to operate in Bolivia until recently have been small ones in the Potosí area (1920-1932) and the Huanuni dredge (1930-1949); a gold dredge has been working in the Alto Beni area since 1958. Since 1967, however, a large dredge has been working the alluvium and water-sorted moraines south of Oruro; these deposits originated in the lodes outcropping in the Avicaya mountains which have themselves been mined since the 1880s. The dredge previously operated in the Californian goldfields before being laboriously dismantled, shipped to Antofagasta, carried by the train load to its new site, and re-assembled there, the whole process taking two years. The dredge can scoop to depths of 30 m. The ore is milled and concentrated on the spot and blended to a 40 per cent tin content; it was anticipated that in 1969 over 1,000 tons of tin, or 3-4 per cent of Bolivia's tin production, would come from this source (Photograph 2a).

The Avicaya dredging operations give employment to about 400 people, but the underground mines require far more labour. In 1962 about 7,500 men and women were employed mining and milling tin ore at Llallagua-Catavi and the figure is probably only slightly less today. The six leading mines probably employed about 15,000 people in 1969. In 1967, the large and medium-sized mines, producing five-sixths of Bolivia's tin between them, employed about 26,500 people; this figure is half the total number of declared miners in the country. It can be calculated that annual productivity in the dredging operations at $2\frac{1}{2}$ tons of tin per man is expected to be three times the figure (five-sixths tons per man) in the medium and large-size mines.

Smelting

Almost all Bolivia's tin concentrates are smelted abroad; in 1967 only 1,000 tons of tin, under 4 per cent of total production, were smelted at home. The bulk of the concentrates was smelted in Europe, almost entirely in Britain, and the rest in the United States. Thus the tin content travels from Bolivia to the smelters as relatively low-grade concentrate, every ton of tin carried having to bear the costs of two tons of gangue. This is an important consideration for the journey is long and broken. The concentrates have to travel hundreds of kilometres across very rugged country to reach the Pacific in a non-Bolivian port still over ten thousand kilometres from their usual destination.

Most of the large mills are on the railway since the railway system of Western Bolivia was built largely to serve the mines. Some concentrates are brought to the nearest rail point by truck, others still arrive by mule and llama train. There are several alternative railway routes to the sea (FIG. 2). The traditional route has been south-eastwards to Antofagasta in Chile, using the railway line which is still British-owned on the Chilean side but which, on the Bolivian, was nationalized in 1965, though it is run by the British company under contract to the Bolivian Government. Although the journey is a long one (Antofagasta is 940 km from Oruro) the gradient is relatively shallow, the journey unbroken, services relatively frequent, and some of the railway overheads could be shared, initially with the Chilean nitrate trade, latterly with Chuquicamata copper shipments. In the 1960s this old established route was challenged by those to Arica and to Mollendo in Peru. The gradual nationalization of the Bolivian railways since 1950 and the policy of the Peruvian Corporation has led to an adjustment of rate structures so that since the early 1960s it has become cheaper to send all tin concentrates (except those produced south of the Rio Mulatos, the junction for Potosí) to the northern ports rather than to Antofagasta/Mejillones. The route to Arica is the shortest (600 km from Oruro) but also the steepest, and the descent from the Altiplano (4,000 m) is achieved only by racking the line over a 41 km section where gradients reach 6 per cent. The route to Mollendo is easier but longer (1,000 km); the concentrates are sent by rail, sometimes by road, to Lake Titicaca, and there transhipped to the railway head in Peru. Both Arica and Mollendo (including its new outport Matarani) have improved facilities substantially in the last decade. In 1962, 87 per cent of Bolivia's tin was shipped from Antofagasta, but since 1963 the northern ports have drawn more of the traffic and over 45 per cent is now exported via Peru.

Most of Bolivia's concentrate output is smelted at Williams Harvey's (Consolidated Tin Smelters) new smelter near Liverpool; a little is smelted at Capper Pass' (Rio Tinto) smelter at North Ferriby near Hull, some in the Rhineland, and some at Arnhem in Holland. In 1967, some 6,000 tons were smelted at the Texas City smelter in the U.S.A., a smelter built during the Second World War when supplies of tin from South-east Asia were cut off and the Atlantic journey for Bolivian tin was dangerous. This smelter has had a chequered career since the war, handling mainly low-grade Bolivian ores, and has changed hands twice in the last three years. It is now to be used to smelt a variety of other metals, and Bolivian tin concentrates are already of no importance.

Tin has been smelted in Bolivia itself in small quantities since the beginning of the century and a smelter has been operating at Oruro since 1947. Three small smelters were operating in the mid-1960s (Peró, Metabol, Hormet) and they smelted 13 per cent of Bolivia's mine production in 1965. In 1968, however, the Peró smelter was transformed into a volatization plant for up-grading pre-concentrates, and Bolivia will not begin shipping large consignments of metal again until the early 1970s.

10

Organization of Tin Production

Tin mining began to be important in Bolivia in the 1890s, reached a peak production of over 46,000 tons in 1929, crashed during the depression of the 1930s, but recovered to maintain levels of 40,000 tons during the years of the Second World War. Production received a stimulus during the Korean war but slumped to around the 20,000 ton mark in 1960; since then there has been a slow but fairly steady recovery to a current 28,000 tons. For most of this time the industry operated under private enterprise. Most important of the individuals to gain huge personal fortunes from Bolivian tin was Simón Patiño. He was a local man, who acquired the Llallagua rights, developed the mine and built a mining empire which became so large as to be responsible for almost one-half of Bolivia's total tin production before 1952. Williams Harvey became, and remains, a Patiño subsidiary. Two other mining empires became outstanding during the first half of this century: one was the Hochschild group whose holdings included Colquiri and Cerro de Potosí mines, and the other was the Aramayo group with mines especially in the south of the country. In the 1940s about three-quarters of Bolivia's tin exports came from the big three.

The three tin empires became a focus for political discontent and the revolution of 1952, supported by the miners, resulted in their nationalization. The Corporación Minera de Bolivia (Comibol) was established in October, 1952, and the management of the mines of the big three placed in its hands. This was the second state enterprise to become involved in the tin industry: the Banco Minero de Bolivia had been set up earlier to assist small mines and others by the provision of loans. In 1939 it received a monopoly to purchase the mineral output of the small mines, a monopoly extended to all mines not nationalized after the Revolution.

Today, tin production is organized in three different ways. All the major mines and mills belong to Comibol; they produce about two-thirds of Bolivia's tin. After the Revolution Comibol was established as, virtually, an autonomous body. Inexperience, multiple allegiances and rank inefficiency of many of its officers took their toll, however, and in the 1960s its independence was sharply reduced and its operations rationalized. One-half of Bolivia's remaining tin production comes from mines in the second category — the medium mines. These are privately owned mines with a minimum production of 5.5 tons of tin, or its equivalent, per month. Many are relics of pre-Revolutionary days though their number was depleted (from 24 to 13) between 1952 and 1956, that is until the monopoly market enjoyed by the Banco Minero was withdrawn. Today, the International Mining Company (U.S.A.-owned) has highly productive mines at Chojilla and Tanapaca; Fabulosa Mines Consolidated, the only company with British attachments, has important mines at Milluni and Huallatani near La Paz; Estalsa is the company working the Avicaya deposits and is a W. R. Grace subsidiary, with Chase International, Lockheed and the U.S. Steel Corporation having minority holdings; and there are at least sixteen other companies with medium-sized mines, including one

11

with Japanese and another with Yugoslav capital. Their presence is a measure of the way in which nationalization in 1952 was aimed not so much at the industry as a whole as against the three big tin empires. Since December, 1967, the division between Comibol and the private mining companies has become less clear-cut as Comibol has been permitted to enter joint financing ventures, providing it retains a majority holding. The small mines, the third category, which contribute about one-eighth of Bolivia's tin production, are frequently one-man or one-family enterprise. They have long been required to sell all their tin-concentrates to the Banco Minero (although there is a little evasion) whereas until recently Comibol and the medium mines could negotiate their own contracts with the smelting companies. In December 1969, the situation was changed, however, with the granting of a state monopoly on all mineral exports to the Banco Minero.

Recent production trends have varied within each category (FIGURE 4). The small miners have proved most inflexible, and annual production has wavered around a total of 3,000 tons over the last twenty years. The private companies have been the most volatile. An annual production of about 4,000 tons before 1952 became half this figure in 1953 and remained at this level through the 1950s; in the 1960s there was a steady improvement, however, and production now is bigger than at any time in the last thirty years. The story is a different one for Comibol. The Revolution was celebrated in 1953, if the statistics give the full picture, by an output of about 30,000 tons, but after 1953 fell in a drastic and dramatic manner to half its former level. The nadir of production was a little over 13,000 tons in 1960. Production has been recovering slowly since then and reached about 19,000 tons in 1969. In spite of the sluggish behaviour of Comibol, Bolivia as a whole has recovered well from the 1958 world-wide slump in tin production and output has risen at a rate slightly higher than that of the world as a whole. This notable performance has been achieved against a background of intense difficulties, some of which are a permanent feature of the Bolivian scene, others of her own making. It has been achieved also partly through a disregard of the cost of production which, but for massive injections of foreign gifts and loans, would have bankrupted the industry and the country with it.

Some Problems of the Industry

Bolivia has problems at all stages in the production process. At the mine the ore is low-grade and difficult to extract; the concentration plants are often inefficient; the journey to market is long; and many of the ores are expensive to smelt. Nationalization has meant that some of the harsh decisions demanded by economic arguments have been softened by social measures and sometimes balanced by political considerations; these have added to the costs the industry must bear. Costs are lower in the private sector but with a world tin price of about $1.41/lb. in 1968, it is probable that the industry did little more than barely break even. Elsewhere in the world the tin mining companies were declaring handsome dividends.

1a.   A Four-Man Private Mine Working to Depths of 30 m near Catavi

1b.   Tailings Dump of the Llallagua Mine at Catavi with the Sink and Float Retreatment Plant in the Foreground.   (Photo courtesy Tin International).

2a.   TIN DREDGER IN OPERATION NEAR AVICAYA.   (Photo courtesy Tin International).

2b.   GENERAL VIEW OF THE COLQUIRI MINE.   (Photo courtesy Tin International).

One of the most important factors making the Bolivian industry a high-cost one is the low quality of the ore mined. In the private sector there has been some counterbalance to the trend towards lower grade ore since there was some closing of exhausted workings and development of new ones; in the public sector neglect in developing new reserves and a natural reluctance to close old mines (with all the social consequences) has made the problem a serious one. The declining grade of ore detailed for Llallagua may be documented for the other big mines: figures available for Colquiri, Potosí, Tasna, Caracoles and others tell the same story. In 1938 the average tin content of ore coming from the large mines was 3 per cent; in 1950 it had fallen to 1.87 per cent; in 1964 it was only 0.82 per cent. In practice this means that, despite a lower total output of tin, a greater volume of ore is being mined today than ever before. The working out of higher-grade deposits, accelerated by the demands of the Second World War and by the policy of the big three tin barons in gutting their mines before nationalization, has had several repercussions. The higher-grade ores were normally shallower ores and, consequently, cheaper to extract than those ores now mined under more difficult conditions at greater depths; they also tended to be less complex and less sulphide-rich and so were cheaper to smelt. On the other hand, a continual decrease in the quality of ore mined has revived the prospects of some mines where bulk mining methods, as at Llallagua, have become a practical proposition: sampling suggests that an ore of 0.77 per cent tin could be won at Huanuni by block-caving, but tests at Cerro de Potosí are less promising. Old mill tailings, too, become an easily-worked source of tin as what was gangue in the past now becomes of acceptable ore quality today: at many mines 5 per cent of the tin output regularly comes from this source. TABLE 1, below, gives figures for the grade of ore supplied to the larger mills in recent years. The lower the grade, the higher the cost of mining a pound of tin, and the larger the proportion of the total cost falling on this factor. In 1964 37 per cent of the total cost of producing an ingot of Comibol tin was accounted for by labour costs at the minehead; in December 1967 it was 30 per cent. At Catavi-Llallagua (where the grade of ore is below average) labour costs were given as 78 cts. per lb. in 1961 or one-half of all the production costs ($1.58/lb.) at a time when the price of tin was $1.11/lb. The direct relationship between high cost and low grade of ore is shown in FIGURE 6: the four mines with the highest overall costs are the only two where the grade of ore exceeded 1.80 per cent. Information for the private mines is generally not available though the fragments that can be gleaned point to generally higher quality ores. The Fabulosa mines, for example, produce ore which averaged 1.25 per cent in 1967; Berenguela 2.8 per cent in 1965; the Bolívar mine of the Tihua company and the Huari-Huari mine of Consorcio Minera Agricola produced mixed ores containing 2-2.5 per cent tin in 1965. What is clear is that labour is generally more productive in the private mines. Two-thirds of the labour employed by the private mines works underground, in contrast to only one-third of those employed by Comibol. Reasons for this disparity are easy to deduce. In particular, it is widely recognized that in the early days of nationalization large numbers of supernumaries were added to the pay-roll of Comibol through the patronage of the government, of officials, and of the

13

unions.   There were 24,000 employed by the big three at the time of nationalization and by 1956 this figure had been swollen to 36,000; since then the figure has declined to 28,000 in 1961 and to about 21,500 today.   The fall has been forced upon Comibol despite union resistance, by her international creditors; the move began to lose its impetus in 1964 but with the ousting of the M.N.R. government then and its replacement by the military government of General Barrientos the power of the unions was further weakened and contraction in the labour force has continued.   Nevertheless, the power of the unions remains stronger in the Comibol mines than it does in the smaller, private mines.   Further, the more limited objectives of the private mines do not run to the provision of facilities which fall within Comibol's budget; for example, Comibol employs a large number of teachers in the major mining centres.   Whatever the reasons, the net result is that in 1966, man-for-man, the medium mines produced twice as much tin as did the Comibol mines.

TABLE 1

DATA FOR CONCENTRATING MILLS, 1964-67

Mill	Average grade of original ore % Sn 1964	Grade of Concentrate % Sn 1964	Degree of Concentration	Loss of tin %	Mill production, 1967 tons of tin in concentrate
Low Sulphur Content:					
Caracoles	1.55	57.5	x 37	27.3	783
Chorolque (Sala-Sala)...	1.95	51.12	x 26	27.9	988
Huanuni	0.77	36.41	x 47	38.6	1,587
Viloco	1.24	40.89	x 33	44.5	480
Catavi (Llallagua)	0.54	49.75	x 92	54.0	4,994
Morococala	1.21	19.97	x 17	65.7	333
High Sulphur Content:					
Colquiri	0.84	33.66	x 40	49.9	2,040
Japo	1.10	36.62	x 33	50.0	225
Santa Fé	1.11	18.10	x 16	63.1	426
Machacamarca (San José)	1.41	21.55	x 15	57.0	863
Potosí	1.18	20.65	x 18	45.7	3,212
Tasna	1.84	40.28	x 23	56.0	510
Comibol:					
Average	0.81	34.08	x 42	49.1	17,210
Private Mills:					
Huari Huari	2.0-2.5	20% (+Zn)		66	78 (1966)
Tihua (Antequera & Bolivar)	2.0-2.5	12-15% (+Zn)		20	400 (1966)
Berenguela	2.8	30%		60	191 (1966)
Kelluani	1.3				
Milluni	0.9			39	456
Huallatani	1.49				340

Another oustanding factor that contributes to the high-cost nature of the Bolivian tin industry is the extraordinary wastage of tin once it reaches the surface.   Only half the tin that enters the concentrating mills as ore is retained in the concentrates and subsequently becomes tin metal; the rest is lost and discarded with the gangue. No other tin-producing country has such a poor record.   There are several reasons

14

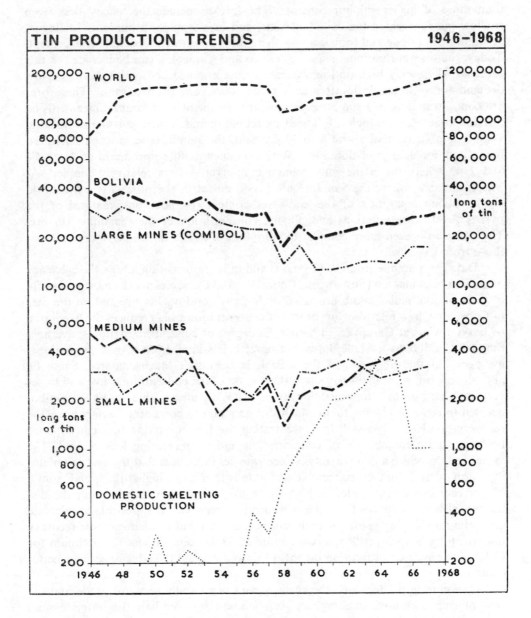

TIN PRODUCTION TRENDS   1946–1968

FIGURE 4

15

for this. The first is the chemical and physical nature of the ores which makes separation difficult. In general, ores of low sulphur content are easier to separate than those of higher sulphur content. The former include the 'pacos' ores from shallow mines working the oxidation zone, and ores from such mines as Llallagua, Huanuni, Chorolque and Morococala, where tin is the only commercial metal present. Today, the tin-wolfram mines, such as Viloco and Caracoles, can be included in this category where only high tin/low wolfram ores are mined and, when there is a low demand for wolfram, little attempt is made to salvage the wolfram. These ores are concentrated in two stages: a preliminary treatment by hydraulic means, using jigs and concentrating tables, followed by remilling and further gravimetric sorting. With a sulphur content above 8 to 10 per cent, the sulphides have to be separated by an additional stage of flotation. With ores such as those produced at Santa Fé and Japo where tin is the only economic mineral, this is relatively simple. At Machacamarca, where the San José ore is concentrated, the process is a three-fold one involving separation of the lead-silver content (by flotation), removal of the pyrites (by further flotation) and, finally, concentration of the remaining tin ore. The situation is even more complicated in mines of mixed tin-lead-zinc ores such as those from Colquiri.

Data for a number of mills (TABLE 1) and other information allows the efficiency of mills to be compared (FIGURE 5). Chorolque and Caracoles are the most successful of the Comibol mills. Both are aided by initially good quality ore and, in the case of Chorolque, by a relatively low degree of concentration which reduces the likelihood of heavy losses; at Caracoles, although the degree of concentration almost averages that for Comibol as a whole, losses are nevertheless kept down to half the national average. At the other end of the scale it is clear that Machacamarca, Santa Fé and Morococala were in a sorry state: the quality of the concentrate is low and losses very high despite low concentration rates. It is significant that in 1968 Comibol decided to cease producing tin at Machacamarca and to concentrate solely upon the recovery of silver. The skill in concentrating ore lies in striking the right balance between an improving rate of concentration and an increasing loss of tin. The incentive to produce a good quality concentrate lies in the fact that the cost of obtaining a ton of tin from a 10 per cent concentrate is four times higher than, and from a 23 per cent concentrate twice as high as, from a 60 per cent concentrate; the disincentive lies in the loss of tin in the concentrating process. It is possible to calculate an optimum shipping grade for each mill bearing in mind its characteristic recovery pattern: for example, in 1965, a concentrate of 33 per cent tin was the optimum for Colquiri; above that proportion the loss of tin outweighed the advantages of a better concentrate.

Concentrate produced by the small miners is generally very low grade and the cost of transportation, smelting, etc. can amount to over half the ultimate sales price. Very primitive concentration processes may still be employed in the small private concerns: hand-picking employs many women and children.

High realization costs add to the problems of the tin industry. Whether the tin travels as low-grade or high-grade concentrates or as tin metal, the journey to market is long.   Freight, insurance and handling rates are lowest per ton for the least valuable low grade concentrates although this is still the most expensive way of shipping the tin content.   The more expensive section of the journey is from the mill to the ship's hold.   Figures quoted in 1967 put the costs of the two legs of the journey to the Williams Harvey smelter in Britain at 4.4 cts./lb. of tin content f.o.b. at Arica and 2.8 cts. from the Pacific port to the smelting furnace, a total of 7.2 cts./lb.; the costs of shipping tin smelted in the Oruro smelter to the New York market in August, 1967, were reported as 8.3 cts./lb. of tin.

Bolivian concentrates are varied in composition and relatively troublesome to smelt; costs can be reduced in some cases by salving some of the impurities and reclaiming such metals as silver and lead.   There is a certain loss of tin in the process which is kept low in the British smelters but which has been substantial at the Metabol smelter in Oruro.   Here smelting costs were 17.6 cts./lb. of tin in 1967 of which 6.5 cts. were due to loss of tin; at Williams Harvey the costs at the smelter totalled only 9.2 cts.   The advantages of a larger smelter, including economies of scale and the greater freedom afforded for blending ores, cannot be gainsaid.

The impact of high mining costs, poor recovery rates at the mills and steep realization costs can be estimated fairly exactly for recent years.   For Comibol as a whole, overall production costs have provided the average figures for the last eight years given in TABLE 2.

TABLE 2

	Cost u.s.$ per lb.	Price Received u.s.$ per lb.	Losses of Comibol in u.s.$ million
1961	1.44	1.11	9.6
1962	1.46	1.12	12.2
1963	1.49	1.14	14.9
1964	1.88	1.55	5.4
1965	1.76	1.76	.03
1966	1.42	1.62	
1967	1.47	1.51	
1968	1.41	1.46	

The difference between cost and price over the years is an indication of the health of this section of the Bolivian tin industry.   Cost data as given for individual mines for 1963 is shown on FIGURE 6.   It is also possible to make calculations of the approximate unit value of tin-in-ore mined from individual mines, taking into account the various costs and losses it has to bear before becoming tin metal.   Assuming a tin price of $1.50/lb., a realistic figure for the late 1960s, the following table (TABLE 3) can be derived.

17

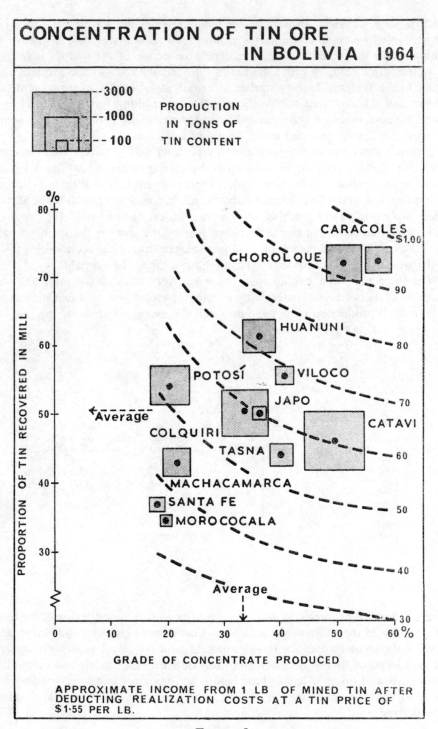

CONCENTRATION OF TIN ORE
IN BOLIVIA 1964

PRODUCTION
IN TONS OF
TIN CONTENT

--3000
--1000
--100

PROPORTION OF TIN RECOVERED IN MILL

%
80
70
60
50
40
30

CARACOLES
$1.00
CHOROLQUE
90
HUANUNI
80
POTOSÍ
VILOCO
70
JAPO
Average
COLQUIRI
CATAVI
TASNA
60
MACHACAMARCA
SANTA FE
50
MOROCOCALA
40
Average
30

0   10   20   30   40   50   60 %

GRADE OF CONCENTRATE PRODUCED

APPROXIMATE INCOME FROM 1 LB OF MINED TIN AFTER
DEDUCTING REALIZATION COSTS AT A TIN PRICE OF
$1·55 PER LB.

FIGURE 5

TABLE 3

Minehead				Approximate value in u.s. cents at the minehead of 1 lb. of tin-in-ore after deducting realisation costs, etc. assuming a tin price of $1.50/lb.	Value of each ton of ore mined in u.s.$
Chorolque	...	...	...	96	42
Caracoles	...	...	...	96	33
Tasna...	...	...	...	58	24
Viloco	...	...	...	73	20
Japo ...	...	...	...	65	16
Potosí	...	...	...	59	15
(Machacamarca)	...	...		48	15
Huanuni	...	...	...	80	13
Colquiri	...	...	...	62	11
Morococala	...	...		36	9
Santa Fé	...	...	...	39	9
Llallagua	...	...	...	61	7
Comibol	...	...	...	64	11
Berenguela *average* ...		...		49	30

The value of a ton of ore mined is an indication of the level to which mining and milling costs must be kept to ensure profitable operation. Since it will be recalled that labour costs are the largest single element entering the cost of mining ore, the importance of high productivity in the mines where the value of ore is low is emphasized.

Prospects for Tin in Bolivia

The short-term prospects for the industry are more hopeful than appeared ten or five years ago and there are a number of new developments which will change substantially the complexion of the industry. In economic terms the labour situation is more satisfactory, new resources are being discovered, more capital is being invested, the wastage of tin at the mills is receiving more attention, and the price of tin is both adequate and reasonably stable. A new development of debatable economic worth but of undoubted domestic political value is the building of the new large smelter at Vinto outside Oruro.

Much of the change of climate has resulted from pressures imposed upon Bolivia by foreign countries as a condition of aid. Between 1957 and 1960 Comibol lost over $30 millions and only vast amounts of American aid kept the country reasonably solvent. Following the publication of a ten-year plan in 1960 which fully acknowledged the disastrous situation of the mainstay of the economy, the Bolivian government entered into agreements with the United States, West Germany and the Inter-American Development Bank — the so-called triangular operation — whereby almost $50 millions was made available specifically to rehabilitate the industry;

since 1961 almost as much money again has been made available by a variety of outside sources. It was an industry badly in need of rehabilitation. Comibol inherited an industry in physical decline whose problems were compounded by nationalization. The flight of foreign professional and technical staff for whom there were no Bolivian replacements, the lack of capital, the heavy taxation imposed to meet the cost of additional (and desirable) social legislation, and abuses of the newly-found power of the labour unions were all unsolved problems in 1960.

The labour problem has been one of the most difficult. For the first five years following nationalization it was almost impossible to dismiss anyone; and it is only at the expense of a gradual disenchantment of labour with the nationalized body that a reduction of labour has been achieved. The history of labour relations in the tin industry is a bloody one and the strikes and disorders at many of the big mines in 1964 and 1965 (and reflected in the high costs of tin production in those years) were no new feature. With the subsequent downfall of the M.N.R. government a harder line has been taken with the miners and, with the help of funds set aside for road building, drawing labour for this purpose, the number of miners is steadily being reduced. A new structure of payments was established abolishing all special payments (with the exception of the bonus for working at over 5,000 m) and a profit-sharing incentive payment was introduced; the mine *pulperías*, providing subsidized goods, have gradually been phased out. These changes have not been accepted without question by the miners. Labour unrest continues to erupt: in July, 1967 between 20 and 70 people were killed in a clash between troops and the miners, and the tin zone came under martial law; the whole country was declared under a state of siege as recently as January, 1969.

Some of the dismissed miners have been able to find work in the private mines, the revival of which has been a deliberate feature of policies designed to encourage private investment. In 1965 a new mining code was introduced which simplified and defined more exactly the relationship between the mines and the state. It also reduced the mining preserves of Comibol and offered certain fiscal incentives to private investors and producers of tin. A new investment code introduced in the same year included the standard inducements to new business that have been a feature of import substitution programmes elsewhere. The results of this programme are making themselves felt. The Avicaya dredge project is backed by an A.I.D. guarantee and registered with INPIBOL (Bolivian Investment Promotion Institute); the El Centenario alluvial deposit 30 kms south of Avicaya near Catavi is being investigated under a U.K. Ministry of Overseas Development grant, and Powell-Duffryn Technical Services is preparing a feasibility report; Alexander Stephen Engineering at Clydeside is building a dredge for assembly in Bolivia; the El Rodeo deposit, which was said in 1965 to be the most important alluvial deposit in Bolivia, is already being explored actively. The Fabulosa mines, expecially Milluni, and the Chojilla and Tanapaca mines have expanded production and are now the most efficient in the country; Trans-American Resources has acquired a large concession and is soon to go into full production. The Kelluani operation is less successful. Comibol has been allocated funds especially to search for and develop new deposits. Results have not been remarkable to date. Funds have been directed at discovering workable reserves of minerals other than tin and it seems that the Tasna-Chorolque area in the south and the Colquiri area in the north (where the Japanese Nitto company also has interests) are the most promising areas.

Perhaps the most intriguing long-term possibility of new tin developments is entirely outside the present tin zone. Placer and lode deposits of cassiterite were discovered in association with low granite masses in the Rondonian territory of Brazil; one of the granite masses extends across the far north-eastern border of Bolivia. So far, although Brazil now produces some 2,500 tons of tin-in-concentrate each year, and tin exports from Rondônia are now more valuable than rubber, a search for economic deposits in Bolivia has gone unrewarded. If tin is found, conditions of working — at 90 m above sea level in the amphibious, forested Amazon basin — will be in remarkable contrast to those normally met with in Bolivian tin mining.

The question of improving recovery rates in the concentrators has attracted considerable attention, but laboratory successes are yet to be matched in the mills. Most of the tin that is lost is in the form of dust, too buoyant to be separated by gravity or flotation. The use of differential milling techniques to cut down the creation of dust grades and of new flotation media promises well, although pilot plants were unsuccessful in 1969; experiments on tailings from the Victoria mill at Catavi suggest the overall recovery rate may be improved by about 10 per cent. The problems faced by Bolivia are not dissimilar to those faced by the Cornish tin miners, and British experts (for example, from the Warren Spring Laboratory and from Head Wrighton Processing Engineers, Ltd.) are helping to tackle them. The United Nations announced in 1969 the establishment of a central plant for re-processing low-grade concentrates, and in 1968 Comibol took over the old Peró smelter and transferred it into a volatization plant for the same purpose. The complexity of the tin ores, their low grade, and the inaccessibility, small size and ephemeral nature of many of the private mines using only primitive concentration methods place a limit upon the savings that can be achieved.

One of the most contentious developments of the last three years has been the decision to build a large new tin smelter at Vinto, near Oruro. A contract was signed by the Bolivian government in 1967 with a Federal German company (Klöckner Industrie Anlagen) and the first part of the smelter was received, amid scenes of official and unofficial jubilation, in Oruro in July, 1968. It may be operating in late 1970 and should be producing 7,500 tons of tin by the mid-1970s with the possibility of expanding capacity later. Bolivia is not the only tin-producing country to break its traditional ties with Europe and build its own smelter — in fact, it is one of the last. A domestic smelter has become a symbol of national pride, and honour is soon to be satisfied. The decision to invest in the smelter has been criticized from both within and outside the country, however, and the economics of the project are not clear, for Bolivian ores are notoriously difficult to smelt. The smelter will concentrate on low-grade ores and will thereby make maximum savings on shipping costs, employment will be provided in Bolivia and valuable foreign exchange saved;

TIN PRODUCTION AND COSTS IN BOLIVIA

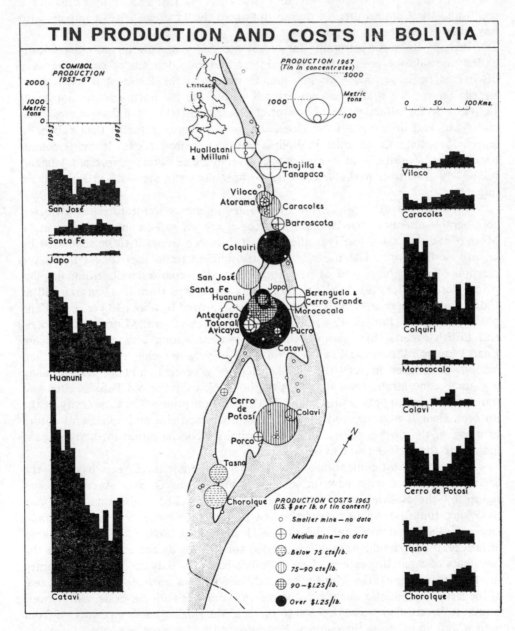

FIGURE 6

on the other hand, the College of Bolivian Economists has received the scheme with reserve and the small and medium-sized miners are suspicious of any extension of government monopoly plans.

The Market for Bolivian Tin

Bolivia sells her tin on the open market and her income depends upon the prevailing world price for tin. In the past, this price has fluctuated widely and Bolivia has been exposed to violent changes in her income, changes over which she had no control. Since 1955, however, Bolivia, in common with all other major tin producing countries and many important tin-consuming countries, has been a signatory of the International Tin Agreement, designed, in part, to mitigate the adverse effects of large shifts in price. The signatory powers attempt to damp down price fluctuations by two mechanisms. A buffer stock of money and tin is jointly owned and used to draw tin off the market when the price seems likely to fall below an agreed figure, and to place tin on the market when shortages seem likely to force the price above an agreed limit; the Buffer Stock Manager has certain discretionary powers. In mid-1969 the buffer stock held reserves of tin alone valued at £11m. The producing countries may also agree to limit exports of tin should supply appear likely to outrun demand. Export quotas were in operation during the twelve months from September, 1968, permitting Bolivia to export about 26,000 tons of tin during the period, or about 17.5 per cent of the world's trade in tin. The internal management of such quotas adds another dimension to the mechanism: in 1969 Comibol was allocated 63.5 per cent of the Bolivian total, the private mines, 22.8 per cent and the small mines (i.e. the Banco Minero) 13.8 per cent.

The Agreement has served Bolivia well: the price of tin is substantially higher than it was in the first year of the Agreement, 1955, and there are grounds for believing the price to be higher than would have been the case if there had been no Agreement. Further, it appears that some of the weaknesses in the Agreement will be less apparent in the future than in the past. Tin supplies from countries outside the Agreement are small; the United States holdings of tin declared surplus to the needs of her strategic stockpile were halved in March, 1969 and now pose a lessened threat to producers; and it is possible that the International Monetary Fund may begin to make available to the tin producing members of the Council resources for contributions to the Council's Buffer Stock which could place the Council in a stronger position to contain speculative market dealings against tin in the future.

Tin and the Bolivian Economy

With the tin industry on a sounder footing than in the recent past, the Bolivian economy is stronger today than it was a decade ago. Paradoxically, the declining importance of the tin industry in the overall economy is also a sign of growing strength. In the very near future, exports of products other than tin may well become as important as tin in the balance of payments account. Symptomatic of this change is the growing involvement of Comibol with other minerals. Today about one-third of Comibol sales are of minerals other than tin; indeed, whereas she only breaks even with tin, sales of copper and silver, bismuth and antimony yield profits (and zinc and lead a loss). Heavy investment in the Pulacayo mine, which was one of the most famous silver producers of South America in the nineteenth century and the first to be linked to Antofagasta by rail, and in Corocoro, which has produced one-half million tons of copper in its time and is only 500 km from Arica by rail, are examples of the new direction of Comibol planning. Private companies, too, are working other deposits. Gold is one of the up-and-coming metals worked not only by the small miners but by large scale operators. It was reported in 1964 that Tidewater Oil was investing $8 million to exploit its gold concessions at Mapiri on the Upper Beni, and the South American Placers Company operating in the same area is highly successful. Shipments of zinc from the remodelled Matilde mine, on the Lake Titicaca-Amazon divide north of La Paz, will begin late this year or early next and will more than quadruple Bolivia's exports of zinc.

The most remarkable impact over the last five years of a private mineral company, however, has been in another direction altogether, that of petroleum. Oil was discovered in the Santa Cruz area in the 1920s, the industry was nationalized in 1936, a pipeline to Arica completed in the 1950s, and a steady export of about 3 million barrels of oil shipped each year between 1956 and 1965. In 1955 the Government allowed foreign companies to explore for oil and Gulf Oil struck lucky, in the Caranda field, north-west of Santa Cruz. In October, 1969, however, the company was expropriated by General Ovando's government, and its installations and assets transferred to the state petroleum agency, YPFB. In 1965 oil exports doubled and in 1969 16 million barrels of oil flowed down the pipeline to Arica. Further developments are likely: a natural gas line being built to the Argentine is due to be completed next year.

The petroleum industry illustrates other aspects of the planned development of the Bolivian economy. Refineries have been built at Camiri, Santa Cruz, Cochabamba and elsewhere, and there is talk of a petrochemical and fertilizer plant in the same area. These would be in harmony with the policy already seen in the commissioning of the new tin smelter at Vinto, of processing at home more of the raw materials which Bolivia produces. These prospective plants also illustrate another aspect of Bolivia's domestic policy: the encouragement of manufacturing industries by an import-substitution policy. The scope for such ventures is obviously limited. The market is small, Bolivia's population is only about 5 million, her per capita income is only about $160 a year, and her raw materials are limited. Although increasing, the manufacturing share of the gross domestic product is only about 15 per cent.

Agriculture continues to occupy most people and to supply 20 per cent of the gross domestic product; it has been one of the most successful sectors in Bolivia's economy since the Revolution.   The transformation of the agricultural system in the highlands and the development of extensive agriculture in the eastern lowlands are well-known features, and their direct impact on the average Bolivian is more important than are any changes in the tin mining industry.

The development of improved communications, essentially roads, has been one of the key features behind the success of agricultural enterprise. Large amounts of foreign aid have been spent, and official plans for the future anticipate continuing high expenditure in this direction. New roads not only provide agriculturists with markets previously inaccessible but also help the miner. Although not specifically directed at the mines, some of the improvement in the tin mining position over the last few years can be attributed to the national investment in improved roads.

In conclusion, it appears that some of the attempts to help Bolivia during the last 10-15 years are bearing fruit. The economy is expanding at about 4-5 per cent per annum and the general standard of living is slowly improving. The dependence of Bolivia on the outside world remains of critical importance: she has received about $400 million in aid of one form or another in the last decade alone. However, she may feel that this form of dependence is at least preferable to her former overwhelming reliance upon the vagaries of the international tin market. Though tin still plays the principal rôle in the Bolivian scene, it does so with the help of a stronger and more active supporting cast drawn from a wider spectrum of the national talents.

SELECTED BIBLIOGRAPHY

Ahlfeld, F. and Schneider-Scherbina, A.
Los Yacimentos minerales y de hidrocarburos de Bolivia. (Ministerio de Minas y Petróleo, Departamento Nacional de Geología, Bol. No. 5 (Especial), La Paz, 1964).

Davila, Michel O.
Primer Simposio Internacional de Concentración del Estaño. (Universidad Técnica de Oruro, Oruro, 1968).

Fox, D. J.
'The Bolivian tin mining industry: some geographical and economic problems'. *In A Technical Conference on Tin.* (International Tin Council, London, 1968), Vol. 2, 357-380.

International Tin Council
Notes on Tin (London, Bimonthly).

Ibid
Statistical Yearbooks and Supplements (London, Annually).

Osborne, H.
Bolivia, a land divided.   (3rd ed., London, 1964).

Wright, P. A.
'Relation between concentrate grade and recovery in some mills of Comibol'. *In A Technical Conference on Tin. op. cit.*, Vol. 2, 403-420.

Zondag, C. H.
The Bolivian Economy 1952-65.   (New York, 1966).

LATIN AMERICAN PUBLICATIONS FUND

Continuing the policy and objects for which the Trust was established of financing, wholly or in part, the publication of original studies which can usefully increase knowledge of the economic, political, social and cultural state of Latin America, the Committee has recommended the publication of David Fox's study of 'Tin and the Bolivian Economy'.

The first publication 'Cities in a Changing Latin America' — two studies of urban growth in the development of Mexico and Venezuela, has aroused a widespread interest which is a source of gratification to those who are so generously contributing to the Fund.

COMMITTEE

The Trust is administered by a distinguished Committee which is made up as follows:

Professor R. A. Humphreys (*Chairman*), Director of Institute of Latin American Studies, University of London.

Mr. David Huelin, Manager, Economic Intelligence Department, Bank of London & South America.

Professor David Joslin, Professor of Economic History, University of Cambridge.

Professor P. E. Russell, Professor of Spanish, University of Oxford.

Dr. Harold Blakemore (*Secretary*), Secretary, Institute of Latin American Studies, University of London.